GIG GUIDE

CD Includes Full-Band
Demonstrations

VOCALS • GUITAR • KEYBOARD • BASS • DRUMS

WEDDING
FIRST SET

The Performance Guide for Bands

ISBN 0-634-02098-6

HAL•LEONARD®
CORPORATION

7777 W. BLUEMOUND RD. P.O. BOX 13819 MILWAUKEE, WI 53213

Visit Hal Leonard Online at
www.halleonard.com

How to Use the Gig Guides

This book is laid out with performance in mind. The setlist we have included reflects a wide selection of the most accessible, "field-tested" material available, arranged for a four-piece band in a sequence that's meant to keep your audience entertained. Use it in rehearsal and performance, following along with the lead sheets and individual parts. Each song in the set includes:

- A two-page lead sheet with chords, melody, and lyrics;
- An intro page with song facts, song form, and performance tips for the full band;
- A page of guidelines for each bandmember, including crucial parts and performance tips for vocals, guitar, keyboards, bass, and drums.

Song intro pages contain some information that might be useful to the frontperson as between-song banter: the story behind the song, when and by whom it was recorded, and so on. Parts and performance tips are written by professional musicians with field experience (not just some guy in a cubicle). If all bandmembers follow their parts in the book and the accompanying CD, and the band rehearses well, you will be gig-ready in no time.

WEDDING
FIRST SET

Contents

About the CD

The audio CD represents a live performance of the setlist by a four-piece group. The songs are played in the most standard, tried-and-true arrangements for guitar, keyboards, bass, and drums, remaining faithful (within reason) to the original versions. In order to cover the vocals as recorded, at least three—if not all—bandmembers should be able to sing. Listen to the recording as you practice your individual parts, paying attention to the feel and the sounds used.

Recorded by the Hal Leonard Studio Band at Beathouse Music, Milwaukee, Wisconsin.

Wonderful Tonight

Words and Music by
Eric Clapton

Bridge

won - der - ful ___ be - cause I see ___ the love - light in ___ your eyes. ___

___ And the won - der of it all ___ is that you

Interlude

just don't ___ re - a - lize ___ how much ___ I love ___ you. ___

D.S. al Coda

Coda

won - der - ful ___ to - night." ___

Outro

Oh, my dar - ling, you ___ are ___ won - der - ful ___ to - night. ___

rit.

2. We go to a party and ev'ryone turns to see
   This beautiful lady that's walkin' around with me.
   And then she asks me, "Do you feel alright?"
   And I say, "Yes, I feel wonderful tonight."

3. It's time to go home now and I've got an achin' head.
   So I give her the car keys and then she helps me to bed.
   And then I tell her, as I turn out the lights,
   I say, "My darling, you are wonderful tonight."

Overview

"Wonderful Tonight" appeared on Eric Clapton's 1977 release *Slowhand*, his first platinum-selling album. It reached #16 on the *Billboard* charts and has since become a pop ballad standard.

A beautiful love song, "Wonderful Tonight" is an ideal tune with which to begin your first set. As a ballad, it gently warms up your audience; it tells the guests that the next phase of the reception has begun—that is, it's time to dance. It also welcomes all ages and abilities out onto the floor, setting the night in motion. The tempo is a laid-back 95 beats per minute—keep it steady!

Another benefit of opening with a ballad is that it's a good soundcheck for the band. With a slow song, it's easier to confirm that each member is in tune, in time, and at the right volume. Following is a checklist of potential trouble spots. Be sure that you've accounted for each during setup:

• Each instrument is properly tuned.

• Each instrument is at the proper volume.

• Lights work and are properly aimed.

• The vocals are clear in the mix.

• Monitors are working and at the right volume levels (if in use).

• Harmony vocals are in tune and properly balanced with the lead vocal.

• The view of the lead singer isn't blocked by other band members.

Section	Length	1st Chord
Intro	8 bars	G
Verse 1	8 bars	G
Chorus	10 bars	C
Verse 2	8 bars	G
Chorus	8 bars	C
Bridge	8 bars	C
Interlude	8 bars	G
Verse 3	8 bars	G
Chorus	10 bars	C
Outro	9 bars	G

Lead Vocal

Range: G to E

Backing Vocals

Chorus

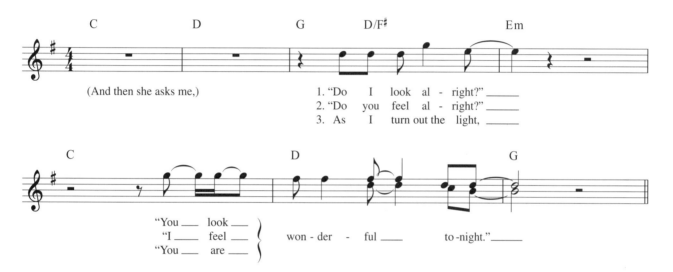

Bridge

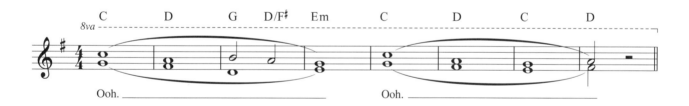

PERFORMANCE TIPS

- Face the audience as you sing.

- Are your vocals clear to you in the monitors?

- Can you hear the backing vocals clearly?

- Can backing vocalists hear themselves and the lead vocal in their monitors?

- Make sure you're enunciating clearly so that the audience can understand the lyrics.

- Sing quietly, introspectively.

- During coda, vocal dips down to E. This note is ornamental; a G note could be substituted.

Guitar

Main Lick: Intro, Interlude, Outro

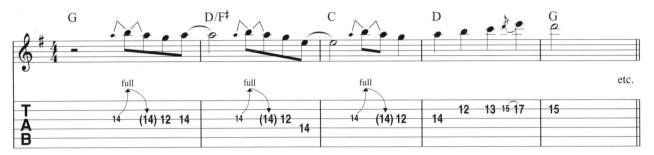

Chords: Verse/Chorus/Bridge

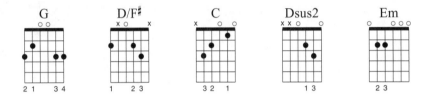

Fill: End of Chorus 2

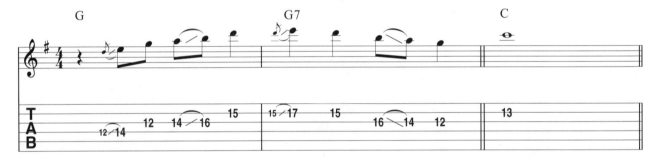

G Major Pentatonic Scale

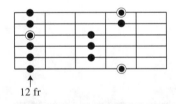

PERFORMANCE TIPS

- Use a Strat-style guitar with pickup in neck position.

- Dial in a clean tone, with reverb (no distortion).

- Be sure to keep bends in tune when playing the main lick.

- Sustain main lick over first chord in verse, then enter at D/F♯ chord (turn volume down).

- During verse and chorus, arpeggiate chords in eighth notes.

- Play fill after second chorus, to the bridge.

- Improvise fills during coda using G major pentatonic scale.

- Option: add open high E string to D/F♯ chord for an elegant flavor.

Keyboard

Intro, Interlude, Outro

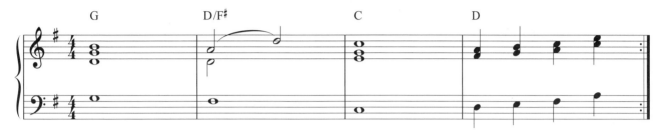

Verse

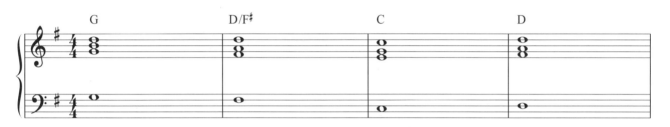

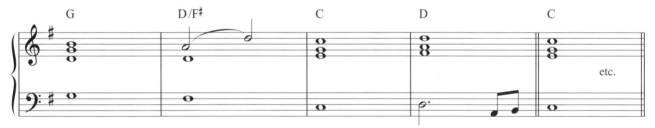

Bridge

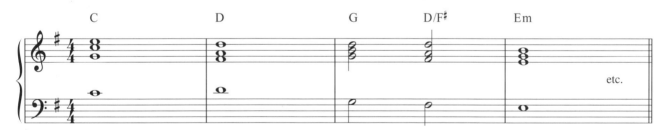

PERFORMANCE TIPS

- Use Hammond B-3 organ or similar sound.

- Set drawbar settings softer than typical rock or blues.

- Use Leslie effect with fast rotation (optional).

- Keep voicings minimal at first; add notes (to build tension) towards end of song.

- Keep volume level below guitar throughout.

- Play slightly louder at intro and bridge.

Bass

Intro, Interlude, Outro

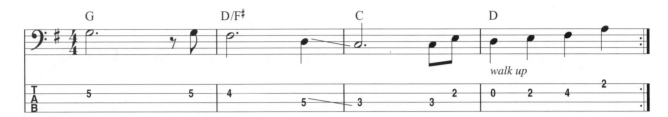

Verse/Chorus

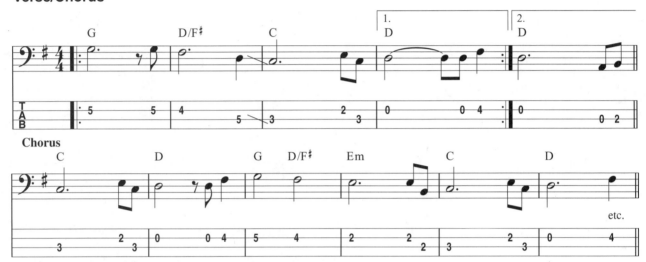

Chorus: 2nd Ending

Bridge

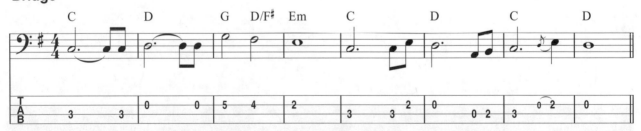

PERFORMANCE TIPS

- Play fingerstyle (or pick gently).

- Use subdued, warm tone—neck pickup, treble rolled slightly off.

- Turn up slightly for intro and bridge, down for verse and chorus.

- Play long notes.

- Walk up to verses (along with guitar), bridge, and ending.

Drums

Intro

Main Groove (Verse/Chorus/Bridge)

Break (to Interlude)

Ending

PERFORMANCE TIPS

- Play kick drum "in the pocket" with bass player.

- Use light touch on hi-hat.

- Strike snare in middle for full, fat tone.

- Play quietly throughout.

- Play intro and bridge slightly louder than verse and chorus.

- No fills throughout.

- Cue ritard at end of song.

My Girl

Words and Music by
William "Smokey" Robinson and Ronald White

Overview

The second song of the night is "My Girl," a 1965 #1 hit by the Temptations that remains an enduring classic today.

"My Girl" relies heavily on vocals. The lyrics narrate a simple story of being in love from the man's perspective. The Temptations sang of "sunshine on a cloudy day," and that theme is something well received by people of all ages. When the singer poses the question, "What could make me feel this way?," everyone sings the answer, "My Girl!" If the crowd is good, sometimes they'll sing louder than the band—now that's song recognition!

The groove on this is a slower, straight eighth-note Motown feel (103 bpm), which is very danceable. The bass and kick-drum intro acts like an anthem, calling people to the dance floor. In this early part of the evening, some people may still want to talk. Volume is still a major consideration—keep it moderate. We want to move the evening into a dance party, but this is not the time to do it. Just groove, and let the singer sell the song to the audience. Watch for the key change at the third verse!

This song appears second in the first set because it is such a "singer's song." You won't be overplaying if you concentrate on vocal harmonies. It's easier to control the level of a vocal performance, because the microphones are so dynamic that you need only move your mouth "off-axis" to drop the volume drastically.

Section	Length	1st Chord
Intro	4 bars	None (C)
Verse 1	8 bars	C
Chorus	8 bars	C
Verse 2	8 bars	C
Chorus	8 bars	C
Interlude	4 bars	None (C)
Bridge	8 bars	C
Verse 3 (Modulate!)	8 bars	D
Chorus	8 bars	D
Outro	17 bars	Dmaj7

Lead Vocal

Range: G to B

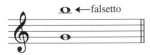

Backing Vocals

Verse 2

Chorus

Bridge

Outro

- Lead vocal adds "melismas" and other vocal ornaments, especially during second and third verses.

- Add slight vibrato on held notes.

- Background vocals should be smooth and even without overpowering the lead.

- Use falsetto voice for high notes.

- Modulate up a whole step (to D) at third verse. .

Guitar

Main Lick: Intro, Interlude

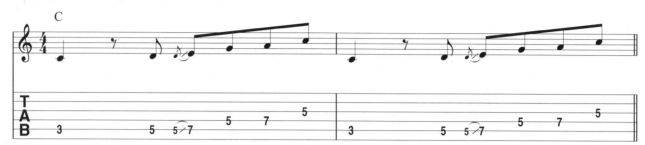

Verse

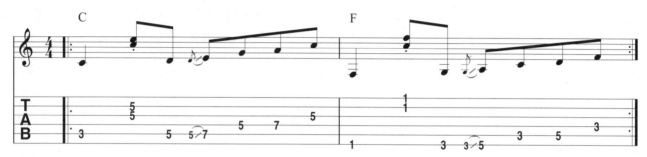

Chorus

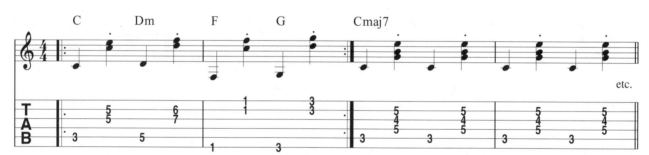

Outro

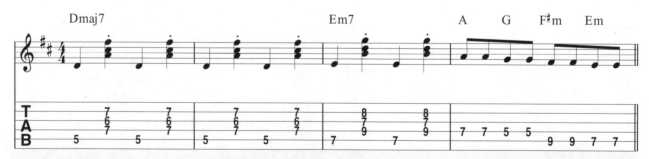

PERFORMANCE TIPS

- Use Strat-style guitar with pickup in bridge position.

- Use a clean tone (no distortion).

- Play all staccato-marked chords as upstrokes.

- Be sure not to rush your chord stabs; they should be locked in with the snare drum.

- At modulation, move all patterns up 2 frets (to key of D).

Keyboard

Verse/Chorus

Verse 2: Brass Line

Strings

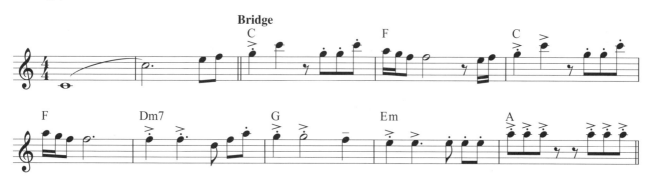

PERFORMANCE TIPS

- Use two keyboards or one keyboard with splitting capabilities.

- Use Rhodes-style piano sound for background chords.

- Use mellow brass or French horn sound for verse 2 brass line.

- At the end of verse 2, quickly change the second keyboard or split-key sound to strings for bridge melody.

- Move all parts up a whole step (to key of D) at modulation.

Bass

Intro/Interlude

Verse

Chorus

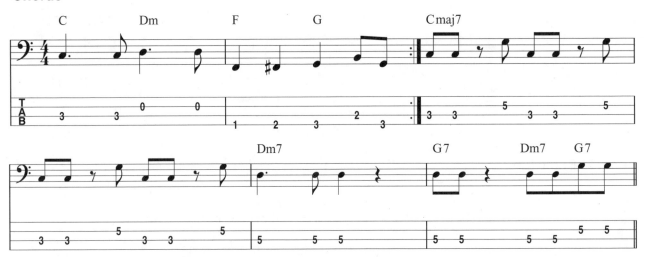

Key Change (End of Bridge)

Walkdown to Outro

PERFORMANCE TIPS

- Lock in with bass drum on the intro.

- Use the eighth-note pattern in the intro as the main groove.

- Use a Fender-style bass with a "fat" tone.

- Repeat the walkdown pattern every fourth bar of the outro.

Drums

Intro

Verse 1

Chorus

End of Chorus Fill

Verse 2 & 3/Bridge

Interlude

Break before Verse 3

Outro

PERFORMANCE TIPS

- Play with laid-back R&B feel.
- Play simple fills.
- Play kick drum "in the pocket" with bass player.
- Cue ritard at end of song with snare flam or fill.

Georgia on My Mind

Words by Stuart Gorrell
Music by Hoagy Carmichael

Intro

Verse

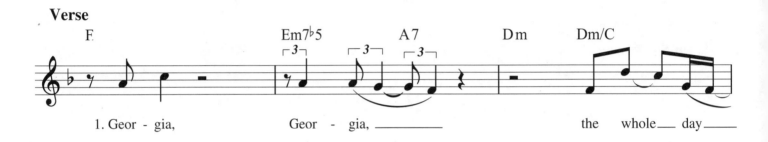

1. Geor - gia, Geor - gia, _____ the whole _ day _

_ through. _ Just an old, sweet song keeps _ Geor - gia _ on

my mind. _____ 2. I say, Geor - gia,
2nd time, Instrumental

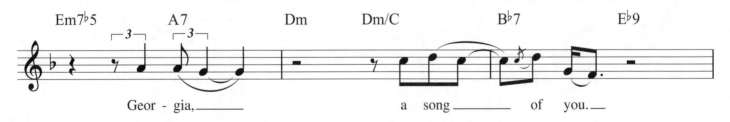

Geor - gia, _____ a song _____ of you. _

comes as sweet and clear as _ moon - light through the pines.

Overview

Our third song is "Georgia on My Mind," a classic originally penned by Hoagy Carmichael and Stuart Gorrell back in 1930. Possibly one of *the* most covered songs of all time, this versatile ballad has been made a nostalgic favorite by Ray Charles, Willie Nelson, and many others.

All of us have experienced homesickness at one time or another in our lives, and to the singer of this song, Georgia is home. As a ballad, this song calls for a lower energy level than "My Girl." It's a couples' song, inviting all those who wish to dance together out onto the floor.

As a band, we are now trying to become an old-style jazz quartet. Our four-piece group switches into "jazz mode," with the bass player emulating (or actually playing) a stand-up bass, the keyboardist switching to an acoustic grand piano sound, the drummer playing with brushes, and the guitarist using or simulating a hollowbody instrument. Tone controls should be down; the groove, laid back.

- Now's the time to double-check: Are guitar and bass in tune? Volumes not creeping up?

- Dynamics should be very quiet throughout the band.

- In jazz-combo tradition, lead vocal should be loudest, followed by piano. All others should be at an equal level of "quietude."

- Swing it, slowly; the whole band should play with an understated triplet feel.

Section	Length	1st Chord
Intro	4 bars	F
Verse 1	8 bars	F
Verse 2	8 bars	F
Bridge	8 bars	Dm
Verse 3	8 bars	F
Verse (Instrumental)	8 bars	F
Bridge	8 bars	Dm
Verse 4	8 bars	F
Outro	4 bars	G7

Lead Vocal

Range: D to F

Backing Vocals

Verses 2, 3, and 4

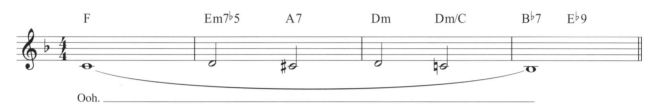

Ooh. _____

Bridge

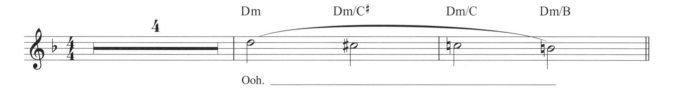

Ooh. _____

Guitar

Chords

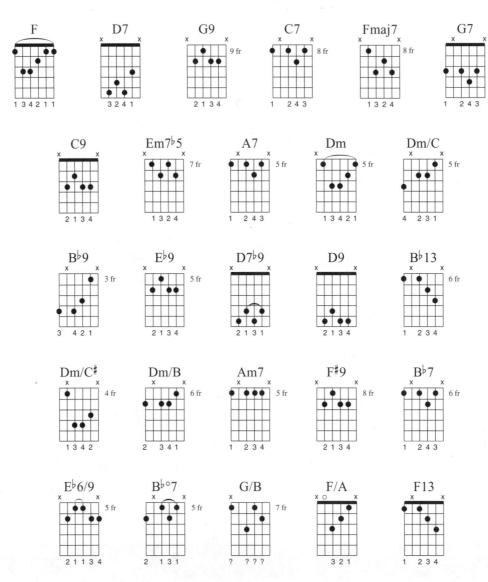

PERFORMANCE TIPS

- Use a hollowbody guitar with pickup in neck position.

- Strum chords on every beat, accenting beats 2 and 4.

- Strum with thumb instead of a pick. When chords change every beat during outro, pluck them with fingers.

- You can substitute a dominant 7th chord for a dominant 9th or 13th (e.g. play A7 for A7♭9, or B♭7 for B♭13).

- Make sure muted notes don't sound when playing broken-set chords.

- Play slightly behind the beat for a lazy, laid-back feel.

Keyboard

Intro

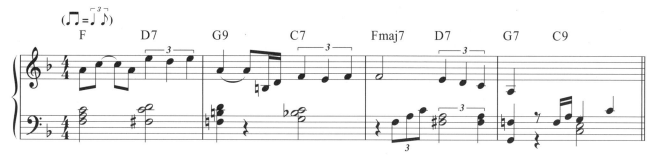

Verse

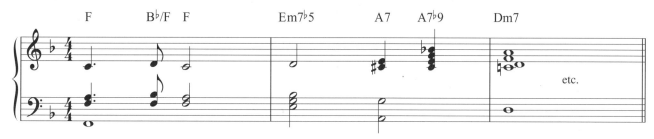

Verse 2 (into Bridge)

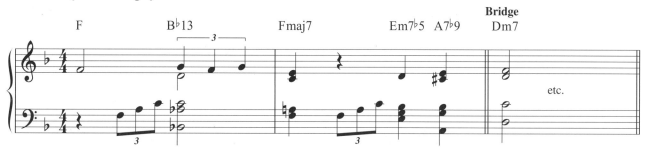

Outro (Last Three Bars)

PERFORMANCE TIPS

- Use an acoustic piano sound. On bridge, switch to a "gospel organ" sound (if available).

- Play "bluesy" licks or short melodic fragments at the ends of vocal phrases.

- Bring up volume and intensity on last six measures.

- Watch vocalist for cue on when to play last chord.

Bass

Intro

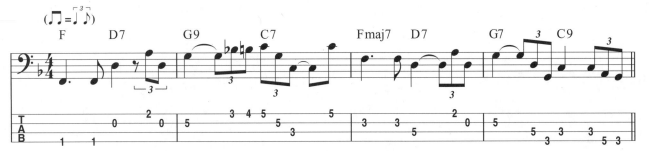

Verse

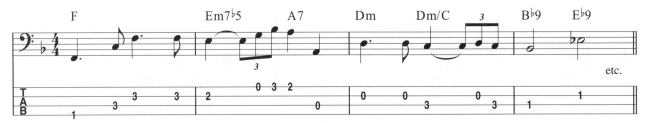

Bridge

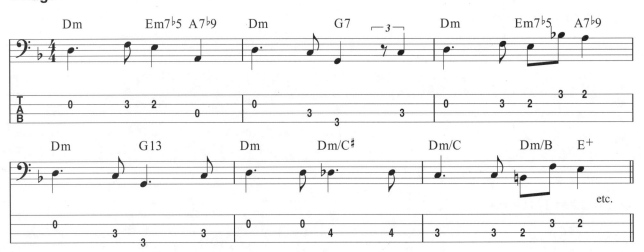

Outro

PERFORMANCE TIPS

- Play with a round, full "string bass" sound.

- Play long notes, use sustain, play slightly behind the beat.

- After intro, use fills—but don't overplay!

- Watch for holds and cutoff on last two chords.

Drums

Main Groove

Ending

PERFORMANCE TIPS

- Play with brushes on white coated snare head.

- Brushes play "swoosh" with quarter-note pulse; improvise throughout.

- Keep time with hi-hat on 2 and 4.

- Play kick very lightly; use only for accenting.

- Cue ritard and cutoff at end of song.

Rock Around the Clock

**Words and Music by
Max C. Freedman and Jimmy DeKnight**

Intro
Moderately Fast Rock

One, two, three o'-clock, four o'-clock rock.

Five, six, sev-en o'-clock, eight o'-clock rock. Nine, ten, e-lev-en o'-clock,

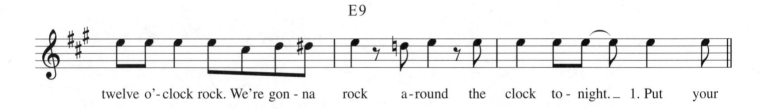

twelve o'-clock rock. We're gon-na rock a-round the clock to-night.__ 1. Put your

Verse

glad rags on, and join me, hon.__ We'll have some fun when the
(2.)clock strikes two, three and four,__ if the band slows down we'll
3.-5. *See additional lyrics*

clock strikes one. } We're gon-na rock a-round the clock to-night.__ We're gon-na
yell for more. {

rock, rock, rock till the broad day-light.__ We're gon-na rock, gon-na rock a-round__

Additional Lyrics

3. When the chimes ring five, six and seven,
   We'll be right in seventh heaven.
   We're gonna rock around the clock tonight…

4. When it's eight, nine, ten, eleven too,
   I'll be goin' strong and so will you.
   We're gonna rock around the clock tonight…

5. When the clock strikes twelve, we'll cool off then,
   Start a-rockin' 'round the clock again.
   We're gonna rock around the clock tonight…

Overview

Now that we've set the mood with sentimental favorites, it's time to bring the energy level way up. With this dance hall standard from Bill Haley and His Comets, we establish the tone of the rest of the evening, what we hope will be the best party of the bride and groom's life. This first smash hit of rock 'n' roll is a great contrast to the jazz ballad "Georgia on My Mind," but that's not the only reason for its place in the setlist. For all the differences between the two songs, the instrumentation is the same: standup bass, archtop guitar, acoustic piano, and drumset (the drummer should pick up sticks again and remove any muffling on the snare).

We've recently seen a re-emergence of swing as a dance movement, and this song falls right into that category. The drums play a swing/shuffle feel, and the bass sticks to a straight "four on the floor" walking line (four quarter notes per measure). The guitar and piano trade "big band hits," playing attacks together in the style of a swing horn section. Even the snare drum gets into the syncopation after the solo, switching to a straight snare rimshot attack on 2 and 4. Vocals should be loud enough to be heard and understood, but not overpowering. Make sure everyone quiets down together after the solo.

Section	Length	1st Chord
Intro	8 bars	A
Verse 1	12 bars	A
Verse 2	12 bars	A
Guitar Solo	12 bars	A
Verse 3	12 bars	A
Verse 4	12 bars	A
Verse 5	12 bars	A
Interlude	12 bars	A

Lead Vocal

Range: A to G

PERFORMANCE TIPS

- Sing short notes, staccato style

- Sing full voice, and use a growl now and then.

- Swing the lines (example: "till the broad day*light*")

- If possible, add short slap-back delay effect to get that "retro" sound.

Guitar

Chords

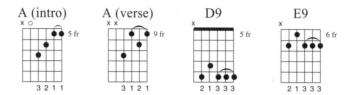

Solo: Opening Lick

Solo: Ending Lick

Outro

PERFORMANCE TIPS

- Use a hollowbody guitar with pickup in bridge position.

- Dial in a clean tone (no distortion).

- Work on alternate picking to get solo licks clean and up to speed.

- Improvise in the middle of the solo in A minor pentatonic.

Keyboard

Intro

Verse

Solo (Comping) **Interlude**

Outro

PERFORMANCE TIPS

- Use a "honky-tonk" piano sound throughout.

- Play with an eighth-note triplet rock feel.

- On verse, try to match chordal rhythms with the snare drum.

- Make sure notes are short.

- On Interlude, bring up volume and match rhythms with the guitar.

- Watch drummer for cutoff on last chord.

Bass

Intro/Verse

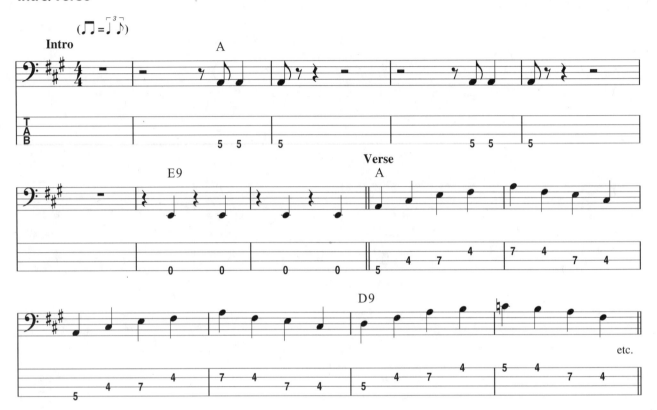

Coda 2 Ending: Walkup

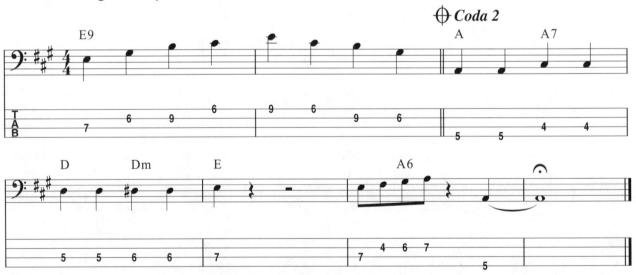

PERFORMANCE TIPS

- Play with a round, full "string bass" sound.

- Stay tight with drums on intro kicks.

Drums

Intro

Verse 1 Groove

Verse 2/Guitar Solo Groove

Fill before Guitar Solo

Verse 3/Interlude Groove

Verse 4 & 5 Groove

Ending Break/Outro Fill

PERFORMANCE TIPS

- Play pickup notes on snare alone (without band).
- Hit snare between rim and head to make it ring.
- Feet play alternating quarter notes between kick drum and hi-hat.
- Play unaccented notes on snare rim much softer than accented notes.

Blue Suede Shoes

Words and Music by
Carl Lee Perkins

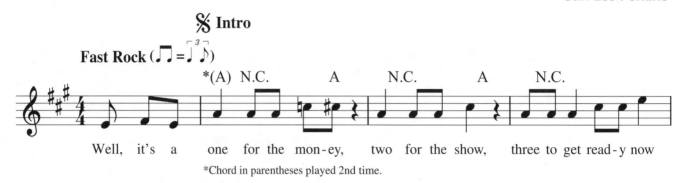

*Chord in parentheses played 2nd time.

Overview

It's no accident that this song strongly resembles "Rock Around the Clock." Another swinging blues-based early rock 'n' roll tune, "Blue Suede Shoes" contains the same type of call-and-response intro between the drums and vocal, with a similar numerical countdown ("one for the money, two for the show..."). The instrumentation is the same, as is the basic song structure. "Blue Suede Shoes" is another instantly recognizable classic, a smash hit that established Elvis Presley as the King of Rock 'n' Roll.

With this song, we continue the momentum we established with "Rock Around the Clock," keeping an even and up-tempo energy level. Since the setup hasn't changed since the last tune, the band can launch straight into this song before anyone gets a chance to leave the dance floor.

Up-tempo swing feels are easily danceable for all ages, and this one will keep things moving.

Once again, we want to simulate a jazz sound; early rock 'n' roll bands were primarily jazz ensembles creating a new style of pop music. The guitar and piano comp in big-band style, the drummer plays rimshots, and the bass keeps walking in eighths. Make sure the band is tight on the intro hits. Dynamics should pick up at the guitar solos, but keep the energy level high throughout.

Section	Length	1st Chord
Intro	4 bars	A
Chorus	8 bars	D9
Verse 1	8 bars	A
Chorus	8 bars	D9
Guitar Solo	12 bars	A
Verse 2	8 bars	A
Chorus	8 bars	D9
Guitar Solo	12 bars	A
Intro	4 bars	A
Chorus	8 bars	D9
Outro	14 bars	A

Lead Vocal

Range: E to A

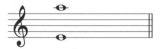

PERFORMANCE TIPS

- Again, swing the lines and throw in a growl now and then ("go cat, go").

- Add short slap-back delay effect to get that "retro" sound.

- Fast, warbly vibrato at phrase ends will make it more Elvis-like.

- Slide up to choice notes ("...*step* on my blue suede...") and down on held notes ("...you can do *anything*...") to give it that rock feel.

- Make sure your vocal is as loud as drummer's rimshots.

Guitar

Chords

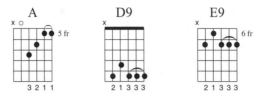

Scale for Solos

A minor pentatonic with added major 2nd, major 3rd, and major 6th

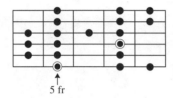

Ending Lick

PERFORMANCE TIPS

- Use a hollowbody guitar with pickup in bridge position.

- Dial in a semi-clean tone that just starts to break up when you really dig in.

- Stay tight with keyboard player on comping parts.

- Improvise solos within the scale shown, using mostly the three highest strings.

- Swing the eighth notes!

Keyboard

Intro

Chorus

Solo Pattern

Ending

PERFORMANCE TIPS

- Stick with the same "honky-tonk" piano sound throughout the song.

- Make sure you play with a shuffle feel.

- Stay tight with the guitar and snare drum.

- Bring volume up slightly during guitar solos.

- Work with guitar player to determine when you will play glissandos.

- On outro, add stab chords at ends of vocal phrases.

Bass

Intro

Chorus

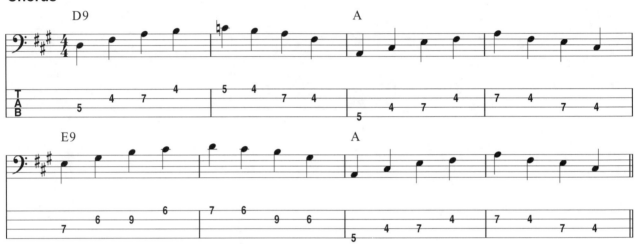

Variation (Solo & Outro)

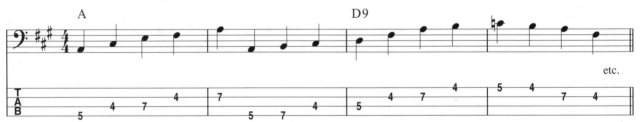

Ending

PERFORMANCE TIPS

- Stick with the same round, fat "upright" sound throughout.

- Walk in fours during guitar solos.

- Don't miss unison line at the end.

- Play on top of the beat—drive the band.

Drums

Intro

Chorus

Lead-in to Verse

Fill into Guitar Solo

Ending

PERFORMANCE TIPS

- Intro is cued off lead vocal.

- Intro riff is played tight with other instruments.

- Main groove is shuffle feel played on half-open hi-hat.

- Ending riff is played in unison with band.

Desafinado

**Original Text by Newton Mendonca
Music byAntonio Carlos Jobim**

Overview

Bringing the energy level back down—but not too far down—and switching from rock 'n' roll to Latin mode, we move next to a bossa nova instrumental, "Desafinado." With this jazz standard from a different part of the globe, we add more variety to the setlist while still keeping it accessible and danceable. This keeps the monotony down and the audience entertained, also giving them a chance to cool down from the high energy of the last two songs. Any ballroom dancers in the audience will step out for this dance-hall favorite.

If we approached "Desafinado" from a traditional Latin standpoint, there might be an entire percussion section instead of just a drumset. In our arrangement, the drummer will mimic the sounds of Latin percussion: the hi-hat acts like a bead shaker playing eighth notes; the snare with the strainer off will sound like a timbale; a cross-stick cup-hand technique on the snare will simulate a pair of claves. The bass and bass drum play together in a repetitive samba-style groove. The piano plays a syncopated Latin jazz line. The lead instrument for most of this tune is nylon-string guitar, which switches to a rhythm role that follows the snare "clave" pattern when the piano solos during verses 4 and 5.

The feel of this tune is light and delicate. Tone settings should be clean, and the band should support the guitar while it plays this sophisticated and beautiful melody.

Section	Length	1st Chord
Intro	8 bars	Fmaj7
Verse 1	16 bars	Fmaj7
Verse 2	16 bars	Fmaj7
Bridge	16 bars	Amaj7
Verse 3	20 bars	Fmaj7
Verse 4 (Piano Solo)	16 bars	Fmaj7
Verse 5 (Piano Solo)	16 bars	Fmaj7
Bridge	16 bars	Amaj7
Verse 6	20 bars	Fmaj7
Outro	7 bars	G♭maj7

No Vocals Throughout

Guitar

Intro

Verse 4 Chords

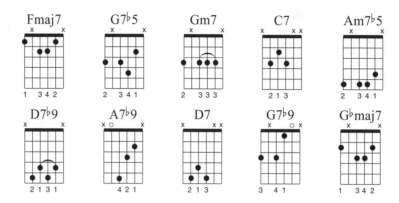

Verse 5 (additional chords)

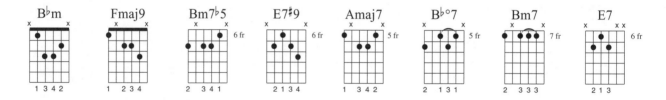

Bridge & Last Verse Chords (optional)

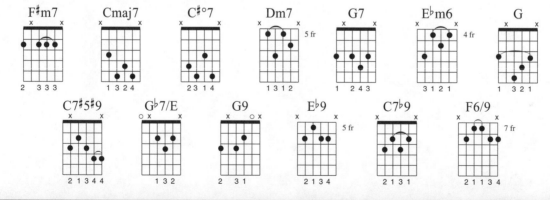

PERFORMANCE TIPS

- Use a nylon-string acoustic-electric guitar, or a hollowbody electric with pickup in neck position.

- Play lead-sheet melody mostly in fifth position, one octave higher than written.

- Tastefully approach some melody notes by sliding up to them from one fret below.

- When comping (under piano solo and at outro), use the same rhythm pattern as in intro. Stay tight with the drummer!

Keyboard

Intro

Bar 11

Verse 1 into Verse 2

Bridge into Verse 3

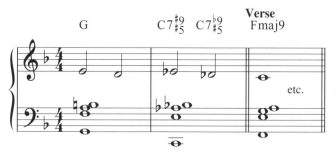

Ending (Last 2 Bars)

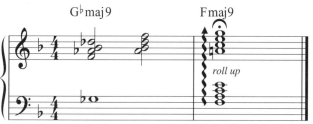

PERFORMANCE TIPS

- Use an acoustic piano sound throughout.

- Add a "mellow string pad" sound to help fill out the sound, if necessary.

- Play with a light, airy Latin jazz feel.

- Bring volume up for solo and back down again to support guitar.

- "Roll up" or quickly arpeggiate last chord.

Bass

Intro

Verse

PERFORMANCE TIPS

- Use a round, mellow tone.

- Play even eighths, lightly.

- Lock in with the bass drum.

- When playing root-fifth patterns, make sure your "5th" doesn't clash with an altered chord (as in A7♭5 or B♭°7).

Drums

Main Groove

Alternate Groove (Bridge & Outro)

Ending

PERFORMANCE TIPS

- Whole band starts together.
- Medium bossa nova/jazz feel using cross-stick.
- Groove changes at bridge from closed hi-hat to ride; when playing the ride, foot plays hi-hat on beats 2 and 4.
- Song ends on beat 1 with full band.

Tennessee Waltz

Words and Music by
Redd Stewart and Pee Wee King

Overview

One of the true tests of a wedding band is the ability to switch musical genres quickly and convincingly. So here we go again: now to a country-bluegrass standard in 3/4 time! Bluegrass, that distinctive American folk music originating in the Appalachians, is closely associated with country. The waltz is a traditional dance form not heard much in pop music today, but still a must-know for wedding bands. The tune should flow like the Danube, with smooth brushstrokes, even and consistent guitar slides, and no jerkiness. Lyrically, this song doesn't exactly express a wedding sentiment, but it's a proven hit nonetheless.

As the band dons new musical hats once again, the keyboardist switches to an accordion sound, the drummer pulls out brushes, and the guitarist dials in a clean, country tone. Lead and backup singers can revive their vocal cords. Notice that this song is shorter than others—if the dance floor fills, you may want to repeat a solo or chorus to stretch it out.

Section	Length	1st Chord
Intro	4 bars	B♭
Verse	16 bars	B♭
Chorus	16 bars	B♭
Verse (Instrumental)	16 bars	B♭
Chorus (Instrumental)	16 bars	B♭
Chorus	16 bars	B♭

Lead Vocal

Range: B♭ to F

Backing Vocals

Chorus

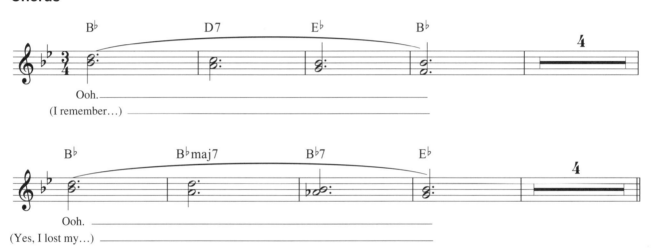

Ooh.

(I remember…)

Ooh.

(Yes, I lost my…)

PERFORMANCE TIPS

- Slide up to select notes ("I was *dancin'* with my *darlin'*…").

- Stress the "r" sound to add a little country twang.

- Start out softer in the lower-register notes, and open up to get louder when the range is higher (…"to the *Tennessee* Waltz…").

Guitar

Intro

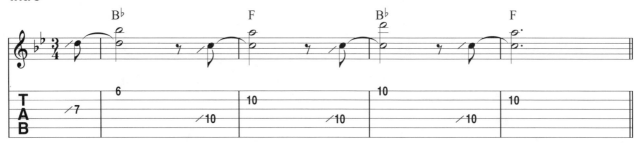

Chords

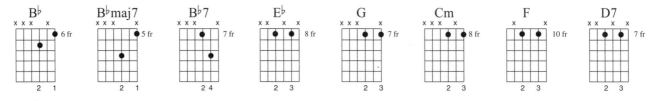

Solo

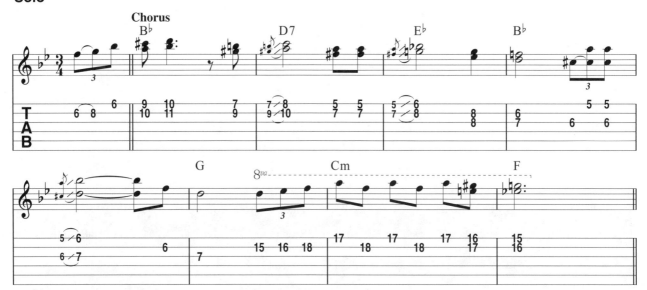

Ending Lick

PERFORMANCE TIPS

- Use a Strat-style guitar with pickup in neck position.

- Dial in a clean tone (no distortion).

- In verse and chorus, use the same technique as intro: slide into arpeggiated chord figures.

- When keyboard solos, fill in with full chords, playing the bass note on beat 1 and strumming on beats 2 and 3.

Keyboard

Intro

Verse

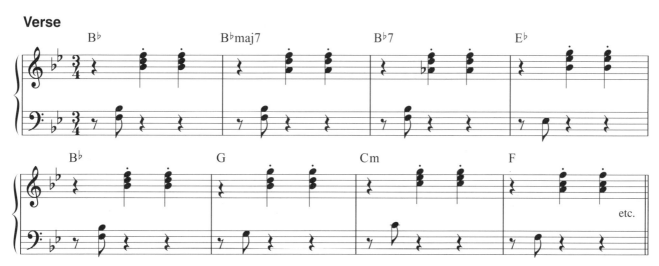

Chorus

PERFORMANCE TIPS

- Use an accordion sound throughout.

- Bring volume up on intro melody, back down when lead vocalist enters at verse.

- On verse, play with a light lilting feel that locks in with drums.

- Elongate the chordal rhythm pattern on chorus.

- Bring volume up for solo and back down when comping beneath guitar.

Bass

Intro

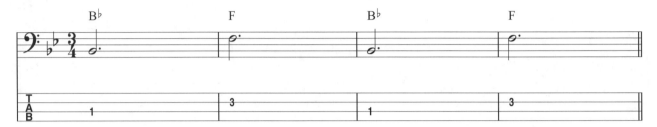

Verse

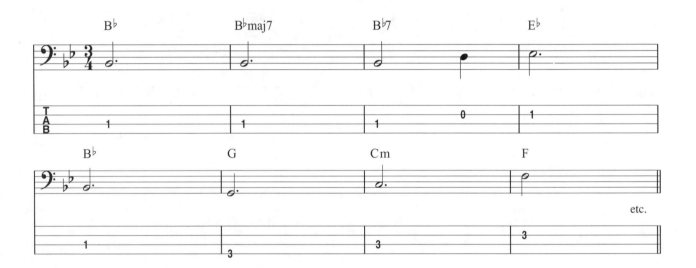

Chorus

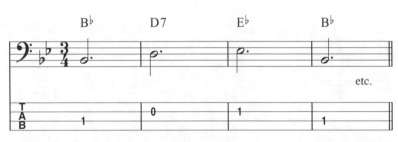

First Ending

PERFORMANCE TIPS

- Play simply, use long notes.

- Use a fat, round tone.

- A walk-up is a good way to connect the first ending to the verse.

- Also use occasional walk-ups from B♭7 to E♭.

Drums

Main Groove

Lead-in to Verse 1

Ending

PERFORMANCE TIPS

- 3/4 (waltz) "swing" feel played with wire brushes on white coated snare drumhead.
- Use no muffling on snare drum.
- Drag brush smoothly on snare from beat 1 to 2.
- Concentrate on consistent shuffled waltz feel.
- End song on beat 1 with band.

Save the Last Dance for Me

**Words and Music by
Doc Pomus and Mort Shuman**

1. You can dance ev - 'ry dance with the guy who gives
2., 3. *See additional lyrics*

____ you the eye; let him hold you tight. ____ You can

smile ev - 'ry smile for a man who held ____ your hand ____ 'neath the

pale ____ moon - light. ____ But don't for - get who's tak - in' you home ____

____ and in ____ whose arms you're ____ gon - na be. ____ 1., 3. So, 2. Oh, dar -

- ling, save the last dance ____ for ____ me. 2. Oh, I

2. Oh, I know that the music's fine
   Like a sparkling wine; go and have your fun.
   Laugh and sing, but while we're apart
   Don't give your heart to anyone.

3. You can dance, go and carry on
   Till the night is gone and it's time to go.
   If he asks if you're all alone,
   Can he take you home, you must tell him no.

Overview

In the fifties, there was an entire movement of vocal groups who fused soul music with popular dance feels and made it more appealing to a young audience. With "Save the Last Dance for Me," we have a great example: R&B-style vocals spun together with a Latin/Carribean feel to make an unbeatable combination. The song's sentiment is universal, and perfect for a wedding.

This arrangement was tailor-made for a four-piece band. The guitarist plays an infectious pattern that really helps push things along when juxtaposed against the staccato bass part and the drummer's clave-style cross-stick snare pattern. The keyboard adds sparkle to the arrangement with a bright vibe sound. The vocals are the real show here. The lead singer is emulating a stylized sound made popular by "doo-wop" singers in the fifties: a breathy sound that takes some practice but is very fun to sing. The backup vocalists are better off without vibrato; harmonies have a tendency to sound out of tune if all voices are vibrating at different rates. Background singers carry lots of weight in this tune: all should be in tune, in time, and at equal volume.

Section	Length	1st Chord
Intro	2 bars	E
Verse 1	10 bars	E
Chorus	8 bars	A
Verse 2	10 bars	E
Chorus	8 bars	A
Bridge	8 bars	B
Verse 3	10 bars	E
Chorus	8 bars	A
Bridge (Instrumental)	8 bars	B
Outro-Chorus	16 bars	A

Lead Vocal

Range: B to F#

Backing Vocals

Verses 2 & 3

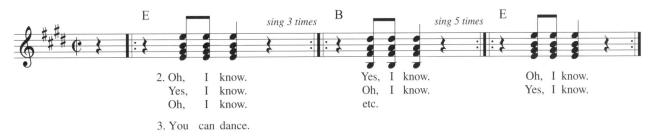

2. Oh, I know.
   Yes, I know.
   Oh, I know.

3. You can dance.

sing 3 times

Yes, I know.
Oh, I know.
etc.

sing 5 times

Oh, I know.
Yes, I know.

Chorus

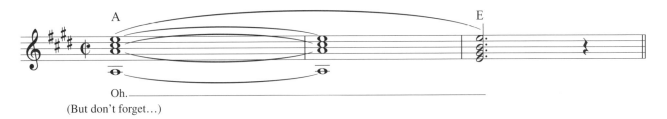

Oh.____

(But don't forget…)

Bridge (and Outro-Chorus)

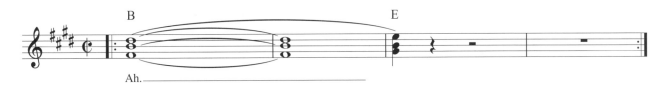

Ah.____

PERFORMANCE TIPS

- Use short notes and lighter voice throughout the verses, stronger and more legato in choruses.

- Lead vocal has wide range; bridge is much lower than chorus.

- Vocals in this song are very rhythmic; make sure all are singing on top of the beat.

- Backup vocals execute a slide in the chorus—see if you can keep it in tune all the way up. If not, split into two distinct notes.

Guitar

Rhythm Pattern

Chords

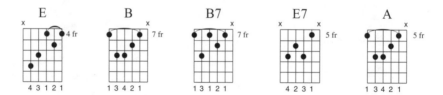

PERFORMANCE TIPS

- Use an electric guitar with pickup in bridge position.

- Stick with a clean tone (no distortion).

- When playing rhythm pattern, use all downstrokes, making sure each note is muted and dynamics are even.

- Play rhythm pattern shown for each respective chord.

- At ending, strum accented E chord in unison with band ("cha-cha-cha").

Keyboard

Intro/Verse

Verse to Chorus Transition

Verse/Chorus (alternate pattern)

Bridge

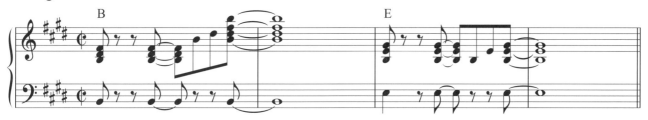

Solo

PERFORMANCE TIPS

- Use a warm vibe sound throughout.
- Play with a Calypso/Carribean feel.
- Make sure volume is below lead vocal. Bring volume up on solo.
- Follow the drummer on accented rhythms at end (play octave E's).

Bass

Intro/Verse

Chorus

Bridge

Ending

PERFORMANCE TIPS

- Keep notes in intro, verse, and chorus short.

- Notes in bridge are more legato.

- Note the different groove in bridge.

- Ending is in unison—follow drummer to keep it tight.

Drums

Main Groove

Ending

PERFORMANCE TIPS

- Band starts together.
- Bossa nova feel using cross-sticking on snare.
- Right hand moves from closed hi-hat to tom on beat 4.
- No fills throughout.
- "Cha cha cha" ending.

Misty

Words by Johnny Burke
Music by Erroll Garner

Overview

Johnny Burke and Erroll Garner wrote this jazz-pop classic, which became a smash hit and signature tune for Johnny Mathis. A must-know for wedding performers, it conveys the "helpless" feeling of being in love and should fill the dance floor with nostalgic and sentimental couples. As we're trying to appeal to a very large demographic, we keep the dynamic levels changing from song to song while remaining in a positive mood. With "Misty," the energy eases back down, and a romantic mood prevails.

The jazz settings used earlier are back, with all the acoustic subtlety we can muster. The lead vocalist is out in front and easily understood. The guitarist uses a mellow archtop sound with reverb, fingerpicking or strumming with the thumb à la big-band jazz. The keyboard and bass sounds are acoustic; the backup vocals, light and airy. The drummer is back to brushes, and the lead vocalist sings with Johnny Mathis-style wide vibrato. In jazz ballad tradition, the drummer acts as more of a color instrument. Bass is now the primary timekeeper, playing steadily and leading the rhythm.

Section	Length	1st Chord
Intro	4 bars	E♭maj7
Verse 1	8 bars	E♭maj7
Verse 2	8 bars	E♭maj7
Bridge	8 bars	B♭m7
Verse 3	8 bars	E♭maj7
Piano Solo (2 verses)	16 bars	E♭maj7
Bridge	8 bars	B♭m7
Verse 4	8 bars	E♭maj7

Lead Vocal

Range: G to F

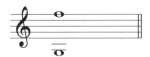

Backing Vocals

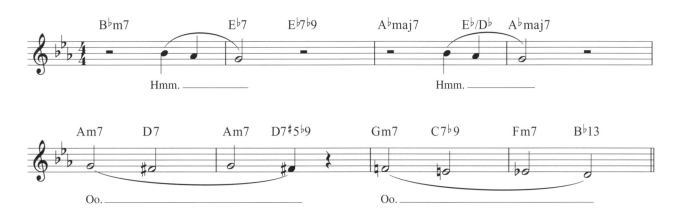

Bridge

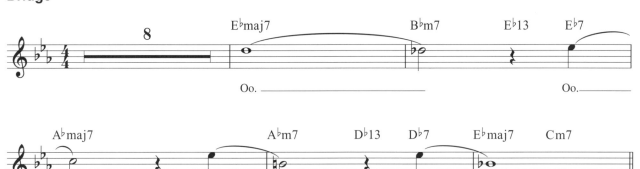

PERFORMANCE TIPS

- Sing in a light, airy "crooner" style.

- Slide down into select notes from the previous note ("Walk my way…").

- Add wide vibrato on held notes at ends of phrases.

- Many liberties can be taken with rhythm, for emotional effect. (Example: "…as a *kitten* up a *tree*." "Kitten" and "tree" arrive early, before the beat.

Guitar

Intro Chords

Verse Chords

  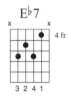  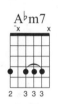

Bridge Chords

 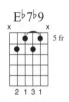 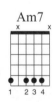  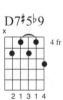

PERFORMANCE TIPS

- Use a hollowbody guitar with pickup in neck position.

- Dial in a clean tone with reverb.

- Play fingerstyle, plucking chords (or strumming with thumb) in quarter notes.

- Emphasize beats 2 and 4.

Keyboard

Intro to Verse

Verse to Bridge Transition

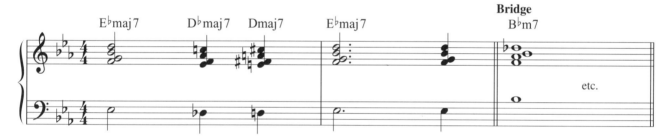

Ending

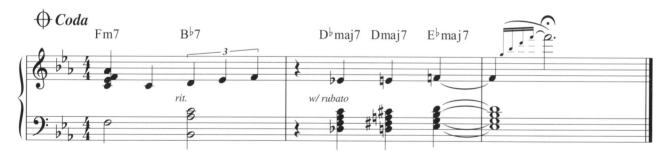

PERFORMANCE TIPS

- Use acoustic piano sound throughout. Add "warm string" pad to help fill out sound, if needed.

- Bring volume up for intro and piano solo; bring back down under lead vocal.

- Play short melodic fragments or licks at ends of vocal phrases.

- Reinforce backup vocals with unison part in right hand.

- Watch other band members to play ritard and last ascending chords of song together.

Bass

Intro

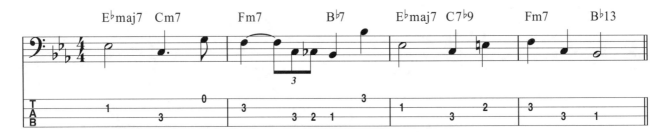

Verse

Bridge

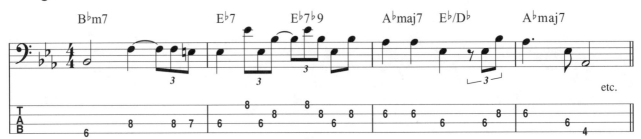

Ending

PERFORMANCE TIPS

- Play mostly half notes; stick to the roots on downbeats.
- Use swing eighths or triplets for fills.
- Lay back, play slightly behind the beat.
- Use a "fat," upright bass-style sound.

Drums

Intro

Main Groove

Coda/Ending

PERFORMANCE TIPS

- Play with wire brushes on white coated snare drumhead.

- Keep time with foot hi-hat on 2 and 4.

- Play kick drum very lightly, use mostly for accents.

- Basic brush pattern on snare plays "swooshes" with quarter-note pulse; improvise throughout.

In the Mood

By Joe Garland

Overview

The second instrumental of the evening is the swing classic "In the Mood." The Glen Miller favorite is a blast to play and to dance to. This big band tune has been a standard since the days when USO bands played it for troops during World War II. No less infectious today than it was then, it is guaranteed to get the dance floor full of swingers of all ages.

This piece isn't without its challenges when performed by a four-piece group. The first and most obvious is that it was originally arranged for a big band, and is best known in that arrangement. The way that we, as a small ensemble, can overcome this is to examine the elements that made this such a great tune and try to emulate those important parts in our thinned-down arrangement.

First, the guitarist handles the intro melody, setting the tempo for the rest of the song. At the beginning of the B section, the piano picks up the well-known theme and the rest of the band joins to establish the swing feel. At this point, the guitar strums in fours along with the walking bass line that keeps things swinging. Note the change in the drummer's pattern when the guitar starts soloing; the cross-stick rimshot pattern keeps the band on track and the groove steady. The piano actually covers the part the horn section would comp if they were here to do it. This is the first song that will feature the pianist as a main melody instrument throughout the song. Enjoy it; the audience will appreciate the band's versatility and ability to cover such a complex arrangement.

Section	Length	1st Chord
A (Intro)	8 bars	N.C.
B (Main Theme)	24 bars	A$\flat$
C (Second Theme)	16 bars	A$\flat$
D (Guitar Solo)	24 bars	A$\flat$6
C (Second Theme)	16 bars	A$\flat$
E (Outro)	4 bars	A$\flat$

No Vocals Throughout

Guitar

Intro (A)

Chords: B (Main Theme)

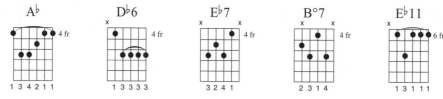

Chords: C (Second Theme)

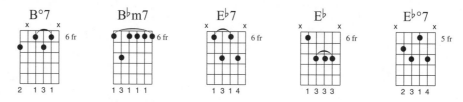

Ending Lick

PERFORMANCE TIPS

- Use a hollowbody guitar with pickup in neck position.

- Dial in a warm, clean tone (no distortion, not too bright).

- Make sure you know the correct tempo to start the tune—get four stick clicks from drummer if necessary.

- After intro lick, strum chords in quarter notes, accenting beats 2 and 4.

- Improvise during the solo using the A♭ blues scale: A♭ minor pentatonic with added flat fifth (D).

Keyboard

Intro (A)

B (Main Theme)

B (last two measures)

C (Second Theme)

C (last two measures)

D (Guitar Solo)

PERFORMANCE TIPS

- Use a bright acoustic piano sound throughout. Option: layer a brass or sax patch on top.
- Melody at "B" is played in octaves. Play a "locked" right- and left-hand technique at "C."
- Bring volume down under guitar solo.
- Play final tag in octaves with guitar and bass.

Bass

A & B

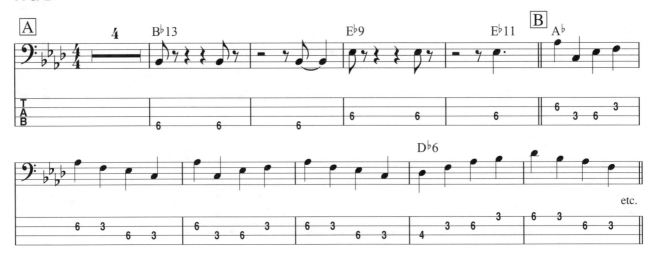

B (last two measures)

C

C into D (Guitar Solo)

E (Ending)

PERFORMANCE TIPS

- The feel is a "swing 4"—use major pentatonic scale under chords.

- Play unison kicks in intro, end of "B" section, end of "C" section, and final ending.

- Go for a round, warm, "string bass" sound.

Drums

Intro

Main Groove   **Guitar Solo**

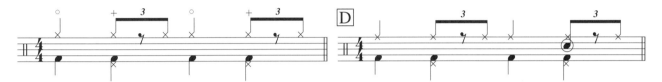

Coda/Ending

PERFORMANCE TIPS

- Play kicks together with band on intro.

- The swing hi-hat keeps time; play bass drum softly.

- Switch to ride cymbal during guitar solo with cross-stick on beat 4.

- Play kicks together with band on ending; choke crash cymbal on last beat.

Could I Have This Dance

Words and Music by
Wayland Holyfield and Bob House

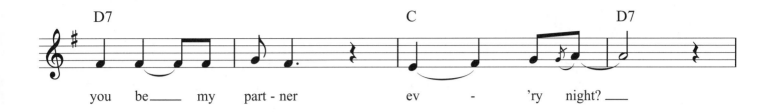

you be___ my part - ner   ev - 'ry night? ___

When we're ___ to - geth - er,   it feels ___   so right. ___   Could

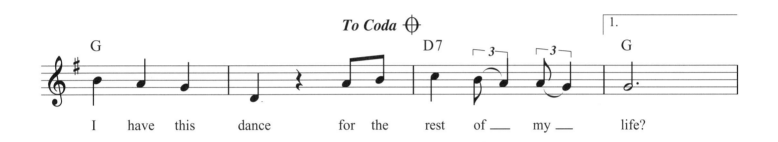

To Coda

I   have   this   dance   for   the   rest   of ___ my ___   life?

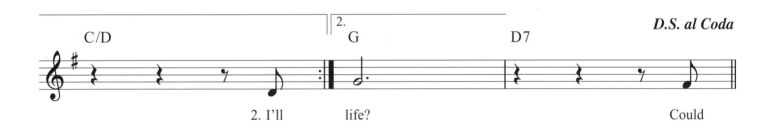

D.S. al Coda

2. I'll   life?   Could

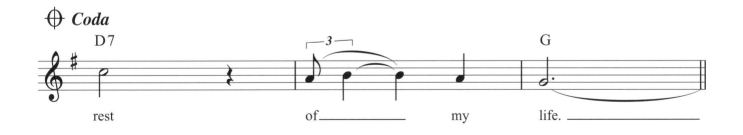

Coda

rest   of ___   my   life. ___

Outro

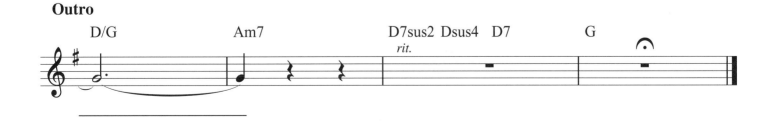

rit.

Overview

It's time to slow down the tempo again with a romantic country-style waltz. Anne Murray had a hit with this pretty song, another wedding standard with a universal message: "Could I have this dance for the rest of my life?" The lyrics are not gender-specific, and the vocal range is compatible with the rest of our tunes.

As you know, waltzes are played in 3/4 time, and it's best to play a slow waltz as smoothly as possible. If beat 1 is too strong, it will not flow like it should or be as danceable.

The guitarist plays the intro lick, then brings the volume down to an accompanying level. Notice the short guitar arpeggio between the chorus and the second verse. It's important for the rest of the band to pause and pick up again on beat 1 of the next measure, for a graceful musical "breath" that leads into the verse. Little breaks like this, when executed together, help give the band a polished, professional sound. Choruses should be slightly louder than verses. Continue building dynamics on the final double chorus.

Section	Length	1st Chord
Intro	4 bars	G
Verse 1	16 bars	G
Chorus	17 bars	G
Verse 2	16 bars	G
Chorus	17 bars	G
Chorus	17 bars	G
Outro	4 bars	D/G

Lead Vocal

Range: D to E

PERFORMANCE TIPS

- Sing calmly; convey a feeling of serenity.

- Slide up to select notes ("I'll *always* remember…").

- Stay on top or a little ahead of the beat.

- Stress the downbeat on select phrases ("*When* we're together…").

- Use dynamics to express the lyrics: sing louder on choruses, build up even more on the final double chorus.

Guitar

Intro Lick

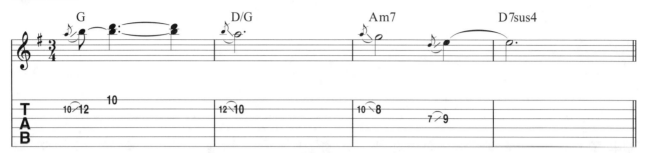

Chords

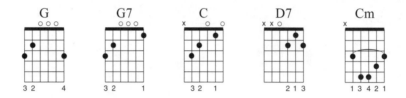

Fill (1st Ending)

Outro Lick

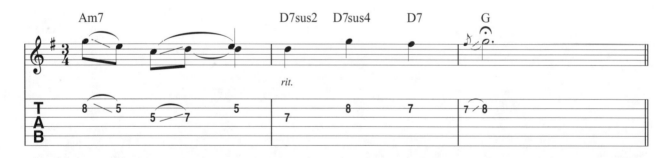

PERFORMANCE TIPS

- Use Strat-style guitar with pickup switch in #2 position (between bridge and middle pickups).
- Dial in a clean tone with slight chorus if desired.
- During verse and chorus, play the chords, picking bass note on beat 1 and strumming on beats 2 and 3.
- Play fill before going into second verse.

Keyboard

Intro

Verse into Chorus

Chorus: Ending 1

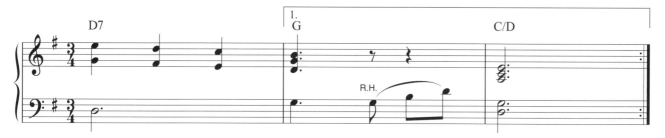

Coda/Outro

PERFORMANCE TIPS

- Use an acoustic piano sound throughout. Add a subtle string pad at final chorus, if desired.

- Play with a "country waltz" feel.

- Bring up the volume for intro and outro, down when vocalist is singing.

- Add Floyd Cramer-style licks at ends of phrases.

Bass

Intro

Verse

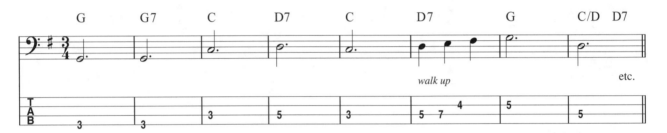

Verse to Chorus

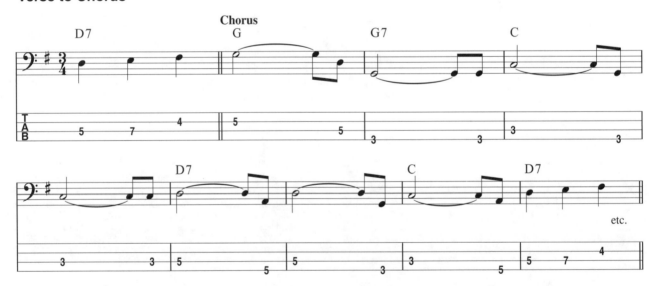

PERFORMANCE TIPS

- Play long notes, lay back.

- Walk up with piano in verse and chorus.

- Keep it simple—don't use excessive fills.

Drums

Intro

Verse

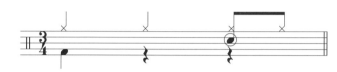

Chorus 1

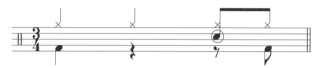

Break before Verse 2

Chorus 2 & 3

Ending

PERFORMANCE TIPS

- Band starts together.

- Intro groove on ride cymbal.

- Verse/chorus 1 groove on hi-hat.

- Chorus 2/chorus 3 groove on ride.

- Cue ritard at end of song.

I Saw Her Standing There

Words and Music by
John Lennon and Paul McCartney

Overview

We close the set with one of the most recognizable songs in rock 'n' roll, the timeless Beatles classic "I Saw Her Standing There." Now's the time to bring the energy level to the highest point of the night so far. As the evening moves on, the music is going to be more consistently "up," and this number is a signal to the audience that the party is just beginning. The bulk of the first set has been deliberately slower-paced, so that the energy can build as the reception picks up. Now we kick it into high gear.

The lead singer counts this one off. The guitarist finds a Beatle-esque tone, the keyboardist sticks with a piano setting, the bass is electric, and the drummer plays a heavy Ringo-style backbeat. The energy level should be high throughout, picking up even more on the bridges and guitar solo. Make sure you can still hear the singer over the high every of the band.

Section	Length	1st Chord
Intro	4 bars (plus count-off)	E7
Verse 1	8 bars	E7
Chorus	8 bars	E7
Verse 2	8 bars	E7
Chorus	8 bars	E7
Bridge	10 bars	A7
Verse 3	8 bars	E7
Chorus	8 bars	E7
Guitar Solo	16 bars	E7
Bridge	10 bars	A7
Verse 4	8 bars	E7
Chorus	8 bars	E7
Outro	9 bars	E7

Lead Vocal

Range: E to C#

Backing Vocals

Chorus

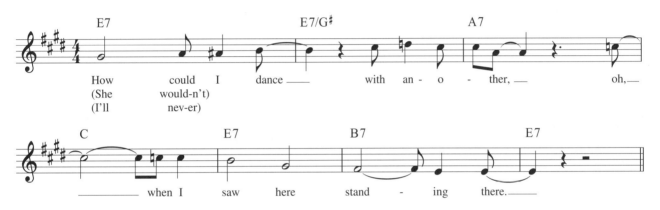

How could I dance ___ with an - o - ther, ___ oh, ___
(She would-n't)
(I'll nev-er)

___ when I saw here stand - ing there. ___

Bridge

Well, my heart went boom ___ when I crossed that room ___

___ and I held her hand ___ in mine. ___

PERFORMANCE TIPS

- Sing full out, put most notes on the beat.

- Many lines include anticipations of beat 1 ("…she was *just* seventeen…").

- Use falsetto voice at end of bridge ("…held her hand in mi-*eeen*…").

- Careful on the scream; with two sets to come, you don't want to scream full out and hurt your voice. (Skip it if necessary.)

Guitar

Intro & Verse

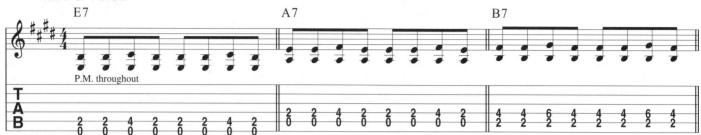

Chorus

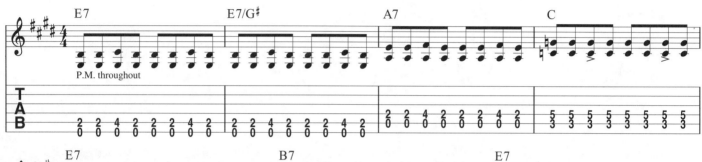

Bridge

Ending

PERFORMANCE TIPS

- Use an electric guitar with pickup in bridge position.

- Dial in a slightly distorted tone.

- Use palm muting throughout (except in the solo).

- Improvise during the solo using E pentatonic minor in open position. Move up higher on the neck for second half of solo.

Keyboard

Intro/Verse Pattern

Verse Chord Change

Chorus

Bridge (2nd time, with gliss)

Ending

PERFORMANCE TIPS

- Use an acoustic rock or honky-tonk piano sound throughout.

- Lower volume when vocalist enters.

- Play with a straight-eighth rock feel.

- Watch drummer for cutoff on last chord.

Bass

Intro & Verse

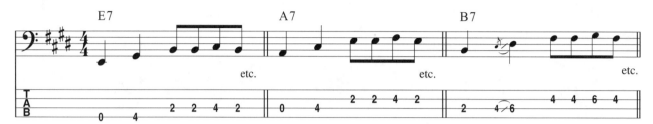

Chorus

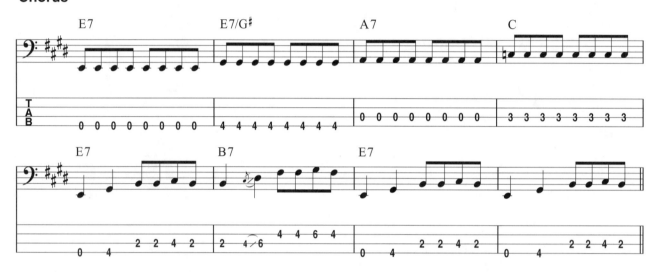

Walkdown (Verse 2 to Chorus)   **Walkdown (Solo to Bridge)**

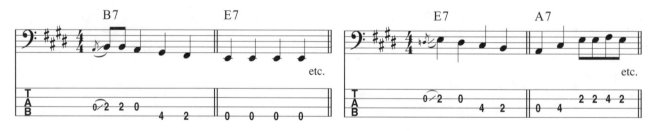

Ending

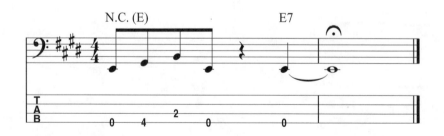

PERFORMANCE TIPS

- Notice groove change in chorus.
- Occasionally add a slide between the first two quarter notes of the bass line.
- Play with energy, on top and driving.
- Add walkdowns at end of verses and guitar solo (during snare fills).

Drums

Main Groove

Sample Fill #1

First and Second Ending (Chorus)

Sample Fill #2

Ending

PERFORMANCE TIPS

- Driving rock 'n' roll beat.

- All fills are snare drum only.

- Ending lick played together with full band.

Guitar Notation Legend

Guitar Music can be notated three different ways: on a *musical staff*, in *tablature*, and in *rhythm slashes*.

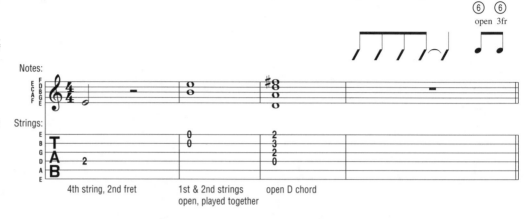

RHYTHM SLASHES are written above the staff. Strum chords in the rhythm indicated. Use the chord diagrams found at the top of the first page of the transcription for the appropriate chord voicings. Round noteheads indicate single notes.

THE MUSICAL STAFF shows pitches and rhythms and is divided by bar lines into measures. Pitches are named after the first seven letters of the alphabet.

TABLATURE graphically represents the guitar fingerboard. Each horizontal line represents a a string, and each number represents a fret.

4th string, 2nd fret · 1st & 2nd strings open, played together · open D chord

Definitions for Special Guitar Notation

HALF-STEP BEND: Strike the note and bend up 1/2 step.

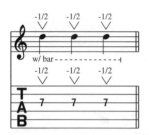

BEND AND RELEASE: Strike the note and bend up as indicated, then release back to the original note. Only the first note is struck.

VIBRATO: The string is vibrated by rapidly bending and releasing the note with the fretting hand.

LEGATO SLIDE: Strike the first note and then slide the same fret-hand finger up or down to the second note. The second note is not struck.

WHOLE-STEP BEND: Strike the note and bend up one step.

PRE-BEND: Bend the note as indicated, then strike it.

WIDE VIBRATO: The pitch is varied to a greater degree by vibrating with the fretting hand.

SHIFT SLIDE: Same as legato slide, except the second note is struck.

GRACE NOTE BEND: Strike the note and bend up as indicated. The first note does not take up any time.

PRE-BEND AND RELEASE: Bend the note as indicated. Strike it and release the bend back to the original note.

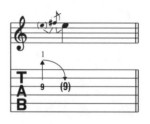

HAMMER-ON: Strike the first (lower) note with one finger, then sound the higher note (on the same string) with another finger by fretting it without picking.

TRILL: Very rapidly alternate between the notes indicated by continuously hammering on and pulling off.

SLIGHT (MICROTONE) BEND: Strike the note and bend up 1/4 step.

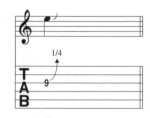

UNISON BEND: Strike the two notes simultaneously and bend the lower note up to the pitch of the higher.

PULL-OFF: Place both fingers on the notes to be sounded. Strike the first note and without picking, pull the finger off to sound the second (lower) note.

TAPPING: Hammer ("tap") the fret indicated with the pick-hand index or middle finger and pull off to the note fretted by the fret hand.

NATURAL HARMONIC: Strike the note while the fret-hand lightly touches the string directly over the fret indicated.

PINCH HARMONIC: The note is fretted normally and a harmonic is produced by adding the edge of the thumb or the tip of the index finger of the pick hand to the normal pick attack.

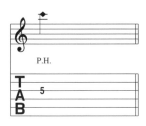

HARP HARMONIC: The note is fretted normally and a harmonic is produced by gently resting the pick hand's index finger directly above the indicated fret (in parentheses) while the pick hand's thumb or pick assists by plucking the appropriate string.

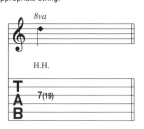

PICK SCRAPE: The edge of the pick is rubbed down (or up) the string, producing a scratchy sound.

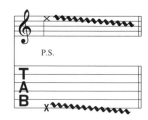

MUFFLED STRINGS: A percussive sound is produced by laying the fret hand across the string(s) without depressing, and striking them with the pick hand.

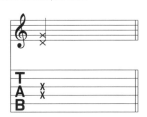

PALM MUTING: The note is partially muted by the pick hand lightly touching the string(s) just before the bridge.

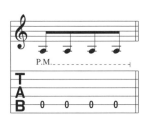

RAKE: Drag the pick across the strings indicated with a single motion.

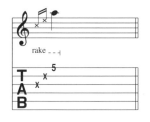

TREMOLO PICKING: The note is picked as rapidly and continuously as possible.

ARPEGGIATE: Play the notes of the chord indicated by quickly rolling them from bottom to top.

VIBRATO BAR DIVE AND RETURN: The pitch of the note or chord is dropped a specified number of steps (in rhythm) then returned to the original pitch.

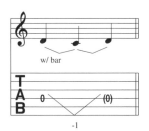

VIBRATO BAR SCOOP: Depress the bar just before striking the note, then quickly release the bar.

VIBRATO BAR DIP: Strike the note and then immediately drop a specified number of steps, then release back to the original pitch.

Additional Musical Definitions

 *(accent)* • Accentuate note (play it louder)

(accent) • Accentuate note with great intensity

(staccato) • Play the note short

 • Downstroke

∨ • Upstroke

D.S. al Coda • Go back to the sign (𝄋), then play until the measure marked "*To Coda*," then skip to the section labelled "*Coda*."

D.S. al Fine • Go back to the beginning of the song and play until the measure marked "*Fine*" (end).

Rhy. Fig. • Label used to recall a recurring accompaniment pattern (usually chordal).

Riff • Label used to recall composed, melodic lines (usually single notes) which recur.

Fill • Label used to identify a brief melodic figure which is to be inserted into the arrangement.

Rhy. Fill • A chordal version of a Fill.

tacet • Instrument is silent (drops out).

• Repeat measures between signs.

 • When a repeated section has different endings, play the first ending only the first time and the second ending only the second time.

NOTE: Tablature numbers in parentheses mean:
1. The note is being sustained over a system (note in standard notation is tied), or
2. The note is sustained, but a new articulation (such as a hammer-on, pull-off, slide or vibrato begins, or
3. The note is a barely audible "ghost" note (note in standard notation is also in parentheses).

Bass Notation Legend

Bass music can be notated two different ways: on a *musical staff*, and in *tablature*.

THE MUSICAL STAFF shows pitches and rhythms and is divided by bar lines into measures. Pitches are named after the first seven letters of the alphabet.

TABLATURE graphically represents the bass fingerboard. Each horizontal line represents a string, and each number represents a fret.

Notes:

Strings:

3rd string, open   2nd string, 2nd fret   1st & 2nd strings open, played together

HAMMER-ON: Strike the first (lower) note with one finger, then sound the higher note (on the same string) with another finger by fretting it without picking.

PULL-OFF: Place both fingers on the notes to be sounded. Strike the first note and without picking, pull the finger off to sound the second (lower) note.

LEGATO SLIDE: Strike the first note and then slide the same fret-hand finger up or down to the second note. The second note is not struck.

SHIFT SLIDE: Same as legato slide, except the second note is struck.

TRILL: Very rapidly alternate between the notes indicated by continuously hammering on and pulling off.

TREMOLO PICKING: The note is picked as rapidly and continuously as possible.

VIBRATO: The string is vibrated by rapidly bending and releasing the note with the fretting hand.

SHAKE: Using one finger, rapidly alternate between two notes on one string by sliding either a half-step above or below.

NATURAL HARMONIC: Strike the note while the fret hand lightly touches the string directly over the fret indicated.

MUFFLED STRINGS: A percussive sound is produced by laying the fret hand across the string(s) without depressing them and striking them with the pick hand.

BEND: Strike the note and bend up the interval shown.

BEND AND RELEASE: Strike the note and bend up as indicated, then release back to the original note. Only the first note is struck.

RIGHT-HAND TAP: Hammer ("tap") the fret indicated with the "pick-hand" index or middle finger and pull off to the note fretted by the fret hand.

LEFT-HAND TAP: Hammer ("tap") the fret indicated with the "fret-hand" index or middle finger.

SLAP: Strike ("slap") string with right-hand thumb.

POP: Snap ("pop") string with right-hand index or middle finger.

Additional Musical Definitions

 (accent) • Accentuate note (play it louder)

 (accent) • Accentuate note with great intensity

 (staccato) • Play the note short

⊓ • Downstroke

∨ • Upstroke

D.S. al Coda • Go back to the sign (𝄋), then play until the measure marked "***To Coda***," then skip to the section labelled "***Coda***."

D.C. al Fine • Go back to the beginning of the song and play until the measure marked "***Fine***" (end).

Bass Fig. • Label used to recall a recurring pattern.

Fill • Label used to identify a brief pattern which is to be inserted into the arrangement.

tacet • Instrument is silent (drops out).

  • Repeat measures between signs.

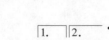 • When a repeated section has different endings, play the first ending only the first time and the second ending only the second time.

NOTE: Tablature numbers in parentheses mean:
1. The note is being sustained over a system (note in standard notation is tied), or
2. The note is sustained, but a new articulation (such as a hammer-on, pull-off, slide or vibrato begins, or
3. The note is a barely audible "ghost" note (note in standard notation is also in parentheses).

Drum Notation Legend

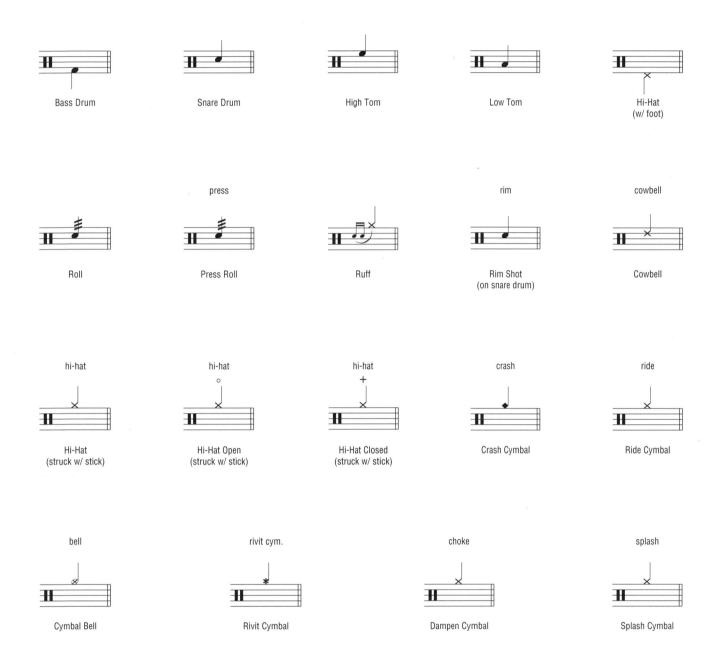